ROSES ARE RED

Sade VandenBurg

BookLeaf Publishing
India | USA | UK

Made with ❤ on the BookLeaf Publishing Platform
www.bookleafpub.in
www.bookleafpub.com

Dedication

to true love, may we find and keep it forever

and

to Oyin, my darling

Preface

I have always believed the soul to be a place of intuitive wild, truths and the deepest love.
May this collection of thoughts and poems flow from my soul to yours, if you wish, as a sign of my love to you.
Thank you for turning each page.

Acknowledgements

My deepest appreciation goes to my readers. Thank you for picking up this book, for considering its pages, for breathing in the words, and for being a part of this (how we say in French: merveilleux, magnifique...) wonderful journey with me.

Thank you to the friends in my life who have pushed me to strive and accomplish my biggest goals and aspirations; who have told me there is nothing holding me back from the dreams I hold in my heart. You are my biggest motivation, my solid rock foundation, and my tether of laughter and fulfillment. I only pray that I return the favor.

Thank you to my mother, for pushing me to write at a young age, continuously and effortlessly supporting my love of reading and writing, and editing my work throughout the years. You are the backbone of my success and the source of adventure beneath my fingertips.

Thank you to the publisher, for the opportunity presented so promptly and swiftly to create my first printed, published and distributed work. You are turning envisage into reality.

how do i tell you

how do I tell you
that you're beautiful,
that I love you
the way you are

how do I put it
so you'll believe me
when I tell you
the world is so warm
with you in it.

roses are red

there was a moment
in the beginning
we hadn't kissed yet
or maybe we had
on the cheek
or the softest way lips meet
I stole a glance at you
while you talked about something
I swear I was listening
but as I soaked in this moment
I just remember thinking
« ah, this was why I liked you,
why I drove out so far
to see you
this was why
I fell for you. »
and I felt it all over again

the leaves

the leaves are changing color
and the flowers are gone,
but that's just a part of winter.

(It's going to be okay)

in my dreams

I began planning,
saving pictures, links,
a list of beautiful places
my favorite of which
was in your arms

light

it's been raining so much lately
the rain always warns you before it falls

is it washing away the roots of the earth
the soot and sand that built up over time
is it a light drizzle
pattering you into calm
letting you breath deeply
letting your shoulders ease

is it a downpour
with such heavy weight, blinding you
can't see past the clouds
constantly wiping your eyes
can't feel more than the numbing and the cold
you're drenched, but not drowning

today the clouds pulled away
puddles lay where the rain fell yesterday
the air is light as i breathe in
moisture droplets hang
at the corners of my eyes
as a reminder
the grass and leaves

begin to sparkle
and beams of sunlight warm my skin

secret

I was hoping you'd kiss me

for no reason at all
we barely know each other
it's just a feeling

tell me everything
while I figure out how to
put myself into words
for you and myself too

you're amazing and so kind
not for me, but for the world
a good soul
I'm sure you have your vices
as do we all
maybe now I'm the red flag
the one who won't
make your parents proud
and maybe a beautiful woman
will come your way
and she will be the one
maybe that's not me

but then why
did I flutter and smile
when you appeared
and reappeared
and again
is it that small of a world
is it coincidence
did our eyes meet because
you were looking for me
or because I was looking for you
or simply because you passed by
as you were supposed to
and all of my hopes are dreams
that will fade with a new day

why was the electricity so hot
in the surges of the elevator
why was I so conscious of the space
between our hands as we walked
why was I searching your eyes
for answers about you and this feeling
hoping it would jump out and be clear
all in those moments
to feel and understand completely
there's more of you that you hold back

I don't know you

but I wanted to know
your hands on my cheeks and my neck
holding my head steady,
planting your lips sincerely on mine,
filling in answers to my questions
making sense of the spaces between us
where words can't be placed quite so eloquently.

if i were free

I'd find purpose by the water,
in the sand, in the sunrise
and in the trees.
I'd meet beautiful people
of different lives and languages
I'd learn new ways
to cook and to create
I'd follow the up and coming
from my island perch
wherever my path has taken me
and when they ask about me,
I could recount the former,
my knowledge of love and life
of cities and treachery
of heartbreak and deepest amity
the previous chapters of my biography
the journey of a ship
that crashed on these shores
and brought me to
who I have become.

wings

when love makes you fly
it is never the same twice
from the moment you take off
it feels like more

more than floating up from the earth
more than a view into your wildest dreams
more than the sunshine on our wings
more than a plunge through warmth and soft air,
into beautiful clouds in the shape of number nine

(on my way to you)

i used to think that

I used to think that
love was unstoppable
when we were young
and love was easy
believing in magic wasn't scary
it was all that was right in the world.
Loving was effortless
being the light wasn't difficult.
I didn't feel the numbness yet
I didn't crawl from darkness each time.
I didn't know any suffering
I knew passion from the greatest things
Purpose for life through love
You could give it all to love
and the world would work around us.
Together nothing was impossible
Together stronger than anything
Nothing could ever break us
We could conquer mountains and build
We could have anything we ever dreamed of
It was like walking on clouds
Not a single thought was in focus
Nothing mattered except everything we felt
and everything we believed in.

Perfection, those feelings.
To let go and be free
Although back then we always felt free
Didn't we?

i don't feel like I'm in love

I feel like painting the sunsets
the way you see it, in millions of colors
and writing about the way we chased it.
I feel like sipping coffee in places with maps
exploring the world and each other,
wandering through cities hand in hand.
I feel like staying under the covers longer
with your arms wrapped around me
taking your hand in the morning
and dancing with you in the kitchen.
I feel like growing into the roots of myself
stretching my all to the moon and sun
because you remind me how to bloom.
I feel like diving into a challenge
floating through with strength and ease
and embracing you at the edge of the waves.

kraken

I spent a lot of time missing you
and I don't want to anymore.
I crave your presence.
I waited long enough.
I enjoy you so much.
a fool to be so vulnerable to you.
I could break so easily,
but here I am.
I melt in your arms
with your lips on mine
and your kisses on my forehead.
I'm aching for your love
and to love you.
to drown in you
would be such a sweet way to go.

royal

if i am in love
then nothing is impossible
I walk on clouds
and breathe fire from my lungs
I conquer mountains and
rule over any village
I wear my crown proudly
flowers and jewels
sprinkle the path behind me
I leave an air of hope
among each path I cross
baskets fill with fruits and health
kisses rain from my cloak
and I perch, legs crossed
at the top of my throne.

my cup of tea

I want to give you
love and peace
kisses on your eyes and cheeks
sweet milk and spice
and a little heat
hold me close to sip so sweet
mix your cube of sugar too
let me lose myself in you
made with love
you're mine to savor
until the last drop
I'll ask one favor
remember the taste
our love so sweet
safe in your heart
until we meet

poison ivy

how I wish
I could not feel
I still want you,
love you and
care for you,
but you said no
its not our time
its not our story
so many reasons to walk away
so finally
I will live my own life
maybe I'll dream of you for a while
I don't want to
but I must continue on now
for me
to take care of myself
in ways you didn't want to
if our time is over
there's nothing i can do
they say life is ahead
with a full heart
not broken
but very cracked
I can survive this

and I can still be happy
I will most probably
think of you
and I will surely
always love you

red string

some loves die
within the first few moments
of knowing them
unaware they
even had a chance
some loves are electric
pulsing through you
all at once
just to leave you
deprived of all energy
some loves are blind
adoring without question
unconditionally pouring
until the well runs
bone dry
some loves are far away
ever reaching and
hoping for more
until lost without
a map to hold
some loves are taken
to the depths of
another world
leaving no chance

of exploration.
you my love
are bound by no means
you triumph time
you conquer dreams
and though there is
no guarantee
I'll find you because
the universe knows
you are my red string

the desert at night

there's a chill in the air
the type that makes your bones ache
and your skin crawl.
your eyes skim across the skyline
its crisp and black and blue,
it begins to shimmer
heap of stars sprinkled effortlessly
by a force only our fingertips beg for.
hands clasped together, head tilted back
the silence calls
bright eyes and dark shadows for company
the mountain a blanket of black
an armor delicate and strong
draped over your shoulders
each step in the sand guided by the moon

sunset

the sunset is different here
I hope you find a love that lets you
fall out of bed laughing
slipping backwards, rolling to the side
tears streaming down your cheeks
a feather tickling your stomach
a smile stretched so far it doesn't fit
jokes that don't make sense to anyone
I hope you find all of these again
because you gave them all to me

flirting in whispers

I love the silent conversations
the raise of an eyebrow
the twist of your lips at the corners
a flash of teeth from a subtle grin
I can feel the whispers
snakes sliding up my arm
delicate and dangerous
from my fingertips to my heart
no words to encapsulate it
my ears tingle from the rush
my cheeks burn hot
my eyes pin to the floor
but impatiently, they meet yours again
the corners of my lips curl upward
and I return the favor to you

roses have thorns

sometimes I say
that I am happy
but I don't always mean it
I haven't meant it in a long time
today I am happy.
truly.
quietly.
subtly.
I feel it in my soul.
I feel it in my bones.
but I won't say it
I won't admit it.
for fear of liking the very thing
that can destroy me.

her essence

you want the essence of a woman
direction, comfort, sweetness, love, tender, support,
adds a bit of something to the room
it's a feeling and I get that now
a caring woman
someone you love and cherish
my best self unhinges without being afraid
I can do that
I have goals now and
I can achieve them all.
I feel it in my soul,
the strength to move forward
I hope it's not too slow for you
I can feel you falling in love
let me show you my greatest strengths
I am unknowingly compassionate,
I write it to remind myself.
I am innately ambitious,
but caring and consistent.
based on experience
my heart does get the best of me
give me time to adjust
and I'll be everything
the world dreams of making me

I pray that our timelines match
I pray that you wont be
missing me too hard
and you'll be happy with everything we have
alone and together we are something magnificent
I look forward to everything this world can give us
boundaries are falling
and I think this could be
something wonderful

stay

i fell in love
when the sunset hit your eyes
so perfectly
the air was golden
and your eyelashes wisped
your green eyes
locked into mine
and in that moment
time stood still
it froze there completely
for me to take it all in
as my heart whispered
you.

www.ingramcontent.com/pod-product-compliance
Lightning Source LLC
LaVergne TN
LVHW041250200726
843507LV00013B/2899